The
Secret
Me

~ A QUESTIONNAIRE JOURNAL ~

Created by:
Shane Windham

NOT INTENDED
FOR USE
BY CHILDREN

At Random

This journal is the property of:

_____

Date begun:

_____

When were you born?

_____

Where were you born?

_____

Can you play chess?
    [   ]yes [   ]no

           Do you believe in love at first sight?
                        [   ]yes [   ]no

Where do you currently live?

_____

When you die, you'd like to have your body:
___Buried   ___Frozen
___Cremated   ___Mummified

Which of your parents named you?

_____

What was your first word?

_____

Would you choose to be immortal, if given the chance?
    [   ]yes [   ]no

           Do you believe in karma?
                [   ]yes [   ]no

At Random

Are your parents divorced?

[   ]yes [   ]no

Do you generally remember your dreams?

[   ]yes [   ]no

How do you prefer your eggs cooked?

_____

Have you seen a ghost?

[   ]yes [   ]no

Have you named a vehicle?

[   ]yes [   ]no

Which of the following bothers you the most:

___Being tickled   ___Papercuts

___Nails scraped on a chalkboard   ___Silence

The most expensive thing you ever paid cash for:

_____

Have you seen a tornado with your own eyes?

[   ]yes [   ]no

Have you been in a long distance relationship?

[   ]yes [   ]no

Have you won a game of pool?

[   ]yes [   ]no

Have you seen a baby being born?

[   ]yes [   ]no

Do you scrub your tongue when brushing your teeth?

[   ]yes [   ]no

Have you been in the ocean?

[   ]yes [   ]no

Have you had a black eye?

[   ]yes [   ]no

Have you hitchhiked?

[   ]yes [   ]no

At Random

Are you good with remembering names?

[   ]yes [   ]no

Are you good with remembering birthdays?

[   ]yes [   ]no

Do you believe in magic?

[   ]yes [   ]no

Do you consider yourself creative?

[   ]yes [   ]no

Do you think you're attractive?

[   ]yes [   ]no

Your profession:

_____

Is your profession what you've always wanted to do?

[   ]yes [   ]no

Have you been more than 20 feet under water?

[   ]yes [   ]no

Your longest friendship has been with whom?

_____

How old were you when you met this person?

_____

Have you ridden on a train?

[   ]yes [   ]no

Were any other names considered when it came to naming you?

[   ]yes [   ]no

If that was a yes, tell us one of those names:

_____

Who taught you how to drive?

_____

Your Lists

People that remind you of yourself:

1.)_____
2.)_____
3.)_____
4.)_____
5.)_____
6.)_____
7.)_____
8.)_____
9.)_____
10.)_____

Phrases you'd like to see on a t-shirt:

1.)_____
2.)_____
3.)_____
4.)_____
5.)_____
6.)_____
7.)_____
8.)_____
9.)_____
10.)_____

Your Lists

Songs you love to sing:

1.)_____
2.)_____
3.)_____
4.)_____
5.)_____
6.)_____
7.)_____
8.)_____
9.)_____
10.)_____

Questions you'd ask on a first date:

1.)_____
2.)_____
3.)_____
4.)_____
5.)_____
6.)_____
7.)_____
8.)_____
9.)_____
10.)_____

At Random

Have you felt an earthquake?
    [   ]yes [   ]no

Have you been overly infatuated with someone?
    [   ]yes [   ]no

How do you think our species will die off?

_____

Have you had a pen pal?
    [   ]yes [   ]no

Have you cried yourself to sleep?
    [   ]yes [   ]no

Is your more photogenic side your right or your left?

_____

Do you currently owe money to a friend or family member?
    [   ]yes [   ]no

Have you worked more than 12 hours in a single day?
    [   ]yes [   ]no

How often do you shower or bathe?

_____

Have you ever tried maintaining a vegetarian diet?
    [   ]yes [   ]no

Do you believe in evolution?
    [   ]yes [   ]no

If you ever ended up on the news, you'd want it to be for:

_____

At Random

You'd do away with which one of the following
weather phenomenon:

___Blizzards   ___Hurricanes
___Earthquakes   ___Tornados
___Floods   ___Volcanoes

If you had time to plan them, what would your last words be?

_____

Do you believe Atlantis ever existed?
     [   ]yes [   ]no
     Have you put money in your mouth since reaching adulthood?
                           [   ]yes [   ]no

You think cheating upsets most people
due to which of the following:

___The fear of losing their lover
___The mistrust it causes
___The inability to control someone
___What it entails physically

Do you believe trees are conscious?
     [   ]yes [   ]no

                        Are you a donor?
                  [   ]yes [   ]no

Why is that?

_____

You believe which one of the following statements to be the truest:

___Nothing is promised, therefore it's every person for them self
___The world owes you something
___You owe the world something
___We're all connected and everything has relevance

When Someone Says, You Think...

Acorns

_____

Afros

_____

Airplanes

_____

Animation

_____

Aquariums

_____

Arrows

_____

Asphalt

_____

Babies

_____

Balloons

_____

Bandanas

_____

Bees

_____

Bells

_____

Bicycles

_____

Billboards

_____

Birdsong

_____

Birth

_____

When Someone Says, You Think...

Bleachers

_____

Blood

_____

Boats

_____

Bones

_____

Boots

_____

Bread

_____

Breath

_____

Brooms

_____

Bubbles

_____

Butterflies

_____

Cages

_____

Calculators

_____

Calendars

_____

Camouflage

_____

Candles

_____

Capes

_____

Ethics and Morality

If you were forced to kill someone, how would you do it?

_____

How would you commit suicide if you were going to?

_____

If you had to say that you admire a serial killer, who would it be?

_____

If you found a wallet filled with money, would you
attempt returning it to its owner?
     [   ]yes [   ]no

Have you taken a stand for someone you didn't even know?
    [   ]yes [   ]no

Would you date a person with a missing finger or toe?
     [   ]yes [   ]no

Do you believe that celibacy is part of
what makes a decent human being?
    [   ]yes [   ]no

Would you shoot your father if it saved your mother's life?
     [   ]yes [   ]no

Would you shoot your mother if she were about to kill you?
    [   ]yes [   ]no

Do you believe everyone is a little racist by nature?
     [   ]yes [   ]no

Have you ever been fascinated by the idea of killing someone?
    [   ]yes [   ]no

Is kidnapping ever condonable?
     [   ]yes [   ]no

Should children under age 12 have to work?
    [   ]yes [   ]no

Should children under age 12 be allowed to work?
     [   ]yes [   ]no

Have you donated blood or plasma?
    [   ]yes [   ]no

Ethics and Morality

Would you kill a child if its living would bring about
the end of humanity?

      [   ]yes [   ]no

      Would you support the idea of all the world's criminally insane
          individuals being sent to live on a deserted island together?

                      [   ]yes [   ]no

Should Americans be free to do whatever they want to themselves,
so long as they aren't physically harming anyone else?

      [   ]yes [   ]no

                      Should all drugs be legal?

                      [   ]yes [   ]no

Do you support the death penalty?

      [   ]yes [   ]no

                Should pornography be legal?

                      [   ]yes [   ]no

Should the possession of firearms by any US citizen be legal?

      [   ]yes [   ]no

          Do you believe that after death you are somehow
                ensured never ending satisfaction?

                      [   ]yes [   ]no

Would you date someone who was
paralyzed from the waist down?

      [   ]yes [   ]no

      Can you think of a moral action performed by a religious person
          which could not be performed by a non-religious person?

                      [   ]yes [   ]no

What is the most important job you can think of anyone doing?

_____

How much do you think that job should pay annually?

_____

How do you morally justify anyone making more than that?

_____

Your Lists

Your ideal mate:

1.)_____

2.)_____

3.)_____

4.)_____

5.)_____

6.)_____

7.)_____

8.)_____

9.)_____

10.)_____

Numbers you'd use regularly on lottery tickets:

1.)_____

2.)_____

3.)_____

4.)_____

5.)_____

6.)_____

7.)_____

8.)_____

9.)_____

10.)_____

Your Lists

Books you'd like to see made into movies:

1.) _____
2.) _____
3.) _____
4.) _____
5.) _____
6.) _____
7.) _____
8.) _____
9.) _____
10.) _____

Topics you avoid in normal conversation:

1.) _____
2.) _____
3.) _____
4.) _____
5.) _____
6.) _____
7.) _____
8.) _____
9.) _____
10.) _____

Your Favorites

Age:

_____

Curse word:

_____

Day of the week:

_____

Exercise:

_____

Firework:

_____

Kind of pillow:

_____

Letter of the alphabet:

_____

Liquor:

_____

Mode of travel:

_____

Month of the year:

_____

Part of a playground:

_____

Piece of clothing:

_____

Planet:

_____

Season:

_____

Sport:

_____

Subject in school:

_____

Time of day:

_____

Type of food:

_____

THIS or THAT

Hot	___OR___	Cold
Rain	___OR___	Shine
Cash	___OR___	Credit
Read	___OR___	Write
A few close friends	___OR___	Tons of acquaintances
White gold	___OR___	Yellow gold
Drink	___OR___	Smoke
Laptop	___OR___	Desktop
Wheat	___OR___	White
Optimistic	___OR___	Pessimistic
Milk	___OR___	Juice
Cake	___OR___	Pie
TV	___OR___	Radio
Microbe	___OR___	Giant
Narcolepsy	___OR___	Tourettes
Sing	___OR___	Dance
Die by electric chair	___OR___	Die by hanging
Star Wars	___OR___	Star Trek
Red wine	___OR___	White wine
Politics	___OR___	Religion
Letters	___OR___	Emails
Yesterday	___OR___	Tomorrow
Fast	___OR___	Slow
Dogs	___OR___	Cats
Internet	___OR___	Phone
Eat	___OR___	Sleep
Live wealthy	___OR___	Die remembered
Vampire	___OR___	Werewolf
Candles	___OR___	Incense
Tip small	___OR___	Tip big
City	___OR___	Country
Fact	___OR___	Fantasy

Your Lists

Things you don't like about yourself:

1.)_____
2.)_____
3.)_____
4.)_____
5.)_____
6.)_____
7.)_____
8.)_____
9.)_____
10.)_____

People who share your birthday:

1.)_____
2.)_____
3.)_____
4.)_____
5.)_____
6.)_____
7.)_____
8.)_____
9.)_____
10.)_____

Your Lists

Ideas which harm the world:

1.)_____
2.)_____
3.)_____
4.)_____
5.)_____
6.)_____
7.)_____
8.)_____
9.)_____
10.)_____

Memorable fortune cookie fortunes you've read:

1.)_____
2.)_____
3.)_____
4.)_____
5.)_____
6.)_____
7.)_____
8.)_____
9.)_____
10.)_____

At Random

Which of your senses are you most fearful of losing?

_____

Have you paid for something which cost more
than five dollars using nothing but change?
      [   ]yes [   ]no
                     Have you been inside of a burning building?
                                   [   ]yes [   ]no

Types of wine you've tried:

___Barbera	___Pinot Blanc
___Brunello	___Pinot Grigio
___Cabernet	___Pinot Noir
___Chablis	___Pinotage
___Champagne	___Port
___Chardonnay	___Red
___Chenin Blanc	___Riesling
___Chianti	___Rose
___Dolcetto	___Sangiovese
___Gewurztraminer	___Sauvignon Blanc
___Grenache	___Semillon
___Kosher	___Sherry
___Madeira	___Syrah (shiraz)
___Marsanne	___Tempranillo
___Merlot	___Vermouth
___Mourvedre	___Viognier
___Muscat	___Zinfandel
___Nebbiolo	

Do you like roller coasters?
      [   ]yes [   ]no
                           Do you sing in the shower?
                               [   ]yes [   ]no

Which of your senses are you least fearful of losing?

_____

At Random

You'd rather attend which one of the following:

___A ballet   ___A play

___A circus   ___A puppet show

___A concert   ___An opera

Have you eaten paper?

    [   ]yes [   ]no

    Have you dated two or more people with the same first name?

                [   ]yes [   ]no

Which of your parents do you resemble the most?

_____

Do you have any children?

    [   ]yes [   ]no

                Do you have a birthmark?

                [   ]yes [   ]no

Do you smoke?

    [   ]yes [   ]no

If you lost all memory of your life, who would you no longer associate with?

_____

                Do you believe there's any scientific evidence supporting astrology?

                [   ]yes [   ]no

Do you believe tarot cards can foretell the future?

    [   ]yes [   ]no

You believe which one of the following statements to be the truest:

___Our existence is unimportant and insignificant

___Life is an experiment in experience

___Consciousness is a paradox

___This life is only preparation for the next

Your Lists

Things which offend you:

1.)_____
2.)_____
3.)_____
4.)_____
5.)_____
6.)_____
7.)_____
8.)_____
9.)_____
10.)_____

Things worth dying for:

1.)_____
2.)_____
3.)_____
4.)_____
5.)_____
6.)_____
7.)_____
8.)_____
9.)_____
10.)_____

Your Lists

Superpowers you'd enjoy having:

1.)_____

2.)_____

3.)_____

4.)_____

5.)_____

6.)_____

7.)_____

8.)_____

9.)_____

10.)_____

Chores you hate doing:

1.)_____

2.)_____

3.)_____

4.)_____

5.)_____

6.)_____

7.)_____

8.)_____

9.)_____

10.)_____

Superstitions

Would you feel uneasy opening an umbrella indoors?
[   ]yes [   ]no

Do you avoid black cats?
[   ]yes [   ]no

Do you believe finding a four-leaf clover is lucky?
[   ]yes [   ]no

Would you feel uneasy putting your left shoe on before your right?
[   ]yes [   ]no

Do you believe a blue flame on a candle indicates
that a ghost is nearby?
[   ]yes [   ]no

Do you believe lightning will never strike a sleeping person?
[   ]yes [   ]no

Do you believe a child born with teeth will be extremely selfish?
[   ]yes [   ]no

Do you believe that a rooster crowing at midnight means
someone nearby has died?
[   ]yes [   ]no

Do you believe a dream catcher will dispose of your nightmares
and cause you to only remember your good dreams?
[   ]yes [   ]no

Do you believe it is bad luck to let a fire
go out on New Year's day?
[   ]yes [   ]no

Do you avoid walking on cracks in the sidewalk?
[   ]yes [   ]no

Do you believe that a person who lived a good life
will find flowers grown on their grave?
[   ]yes [   ]no

Do you believe a seventh son will find more success
in life than the other six?
[   ]yes [   ]no

Do you believe babies born with blue veins across their noses
will not live to be 21?
[   ]yes [   ]no

Do you believe breaking a mirror will mean seven years bad luck?
[   ]yes [   ]no

Superstitions

Do you believe carrying a rabbit's foot is lucky?

[   ]yes [   ]no

Do you believe you can tell the sex of a child by whether or not the mother is carrying high or low?

[   ]yes [   ]no

Do you believe dropping silverware causes company?

[   ]yes [   ]no

Do you believe eating black-eyed peas on New Year's day will bring you luck?

[   ]yes [   ]no

Do you believe half an onion placed under the bed of a sick person will bring about a faster return to health?

[   ]yes [   ]no

Do you believe handling toads will cause warts?

[   ]yes [   ]no

Do you believe it is bad luck for the groom to see the bride before the wedding?

[   ]yes [   ]no

Do you believe it to be unlucky if a flag touches the ground?

[   ]yes [   ]no

Does seeing cows lying down in a field make you think it's going to rain?

[   ]yes [   ]no

Do you believe that getting a chill or goose bumps means someone is walking over the spot which will one day be your grave?

[   ]yes [   ]no

Do you believe it unlucky to count the cars in a funeral procession?

[   ]yes [   ]no

Do you believe it unlucky to leave a clock running in a room where someone has just died?

[   ]yes [   ]no

Would you believe you'll never marry if someone ran over your feet with a broom while sweeping?

[   ]yes [   ]no

Do you believe it's lucky to spill matches?

[   ]yes [   ]no

Your Lists

Must-have items in your home:

1.)_____

2.)_____

3.)_____

4.)_____

5.)_____

6.)_____

7.)_____

8.)_____

9.)_____

10.)_____

Things you don't leave home without:

1.)_____

2.)_____

3.)_____

4.)_____

5.)_____

6.)_____

7.)_____

8.)_____

9.)_____

10.)_____

Your Lists

Things you'd want on a deserted island:

1.)_____
2.)_____
3.)_____
4.)_____
5.)_____
6.)_____
7.)_____
8.)_____
9.)_____
10.)_____

Your previous addresses:

1.)_____
2.)_____
3.)_____
4.)_____
5.)_____
6.)_____
7.)_____
8.)_____
9.)_____
10.)_____

At Random

If you were a rapper, you'd go by what name?

_____

How do you prefer your steaks cooked?

_____

The most memorable untrue rumor ever spread about you:

_____

A party isn't a party until:

_____

Your annual income:

_____

Do you think America's war on drugs is going successfully?
 [   ]yes [   ]no

When a telemarketer calls and you happen to answer
the phone, what do you usually do?

_____

If you could've chosen your name, it would be:

_____

Something people make fun of you for:

_____

You would say you behave mostly like which of your parents?

_____

The most joy you ever derived from working:

_____

At Random

Your blood type:

_____

Your heritage:

_____

Which ethnicity are you most attracted to?

_____

Your weight:

_____

The weight you'd like to be:

_____

Someone you've always wanted to kiss:

_____

Your eye color:

_____

Your hair color:

_____

How many siblings do you have?

_____

Your shoe size:

_____

Your lucky number:

_____

Your Lists

Tattoos or piercings you'd get, if forced:

1.)_____

2.)_____

3.)_____

4.)_____

5.)_____

6.)_____

7.)_____

8.)_____

9.)_____

10.)_____

Things you like to talk about:

1.)_____

2.)_____

3.)_____

4.)_____

5.)_____

6.)_____

7.)_____

8.)_____

9.)_____

10.)_____

Your Lists

Holidays you'd like to introduce:

1.)_____
2.)_____
3.)_____
4.)_____
5.)_____
6.)_____
7.)_____
8.)_____
9.)_____
10.)_____

Your dream vehicles:

1.)_____
2.)_____
3.)_____
4.)_____
5.)_____
6.)_____
7.)_____
8.)_____
9.)_____
10.)_____

The Criminal In You

Have you littered?
    [   ]yes [   ]no

                             Have you been ticketed?
                                   [   ]yes [   ]no

Have you urinated outside of a restroom, in a public place?
    [   ]yes [   ]no

                  Have you driven over the speed limit?
                                   [   ]yes [   ]no

Have you failed to come to a complete stop at a stop sign?
    [   ]yes [   ]no

Have you failed to signal when turning a corner or changing lanes?
                                   [   ]yes [   ]no

Have you used the horn in your vehicle
when it wasn't an emergency?
    [   ]yes [   ]no

                           Have you jaywalked?
                                   [   ]yes [   ]no

Have you been in a public park after hours?
    [   ]yes [   ]no

Have you spent a significant amount of time in a place of business
                            without purchasing anything?
                                   [   ]yes [   ]no

Have you gone through someone's things
without their permission?
    [   ]yes [   ]no

Have you been in a restroom designated for the opposite sex?
                                   [   ]yes [   ]no

Have you spied on someone?
    [   ]yes [   ]no

Have you downloaded anything illegally on the internet?
                                   [   ]yes [   ]no

Have you taken a pill from a prescription
which wasn't written for you?
    [   ]yes [   ]no

                    Did you drink alcohol under the age of 21?
                                   [   ]yes [   ]no

At Random

You believe love has more to do with which one of the following:
___Common interests   ___Physical attraction
___Dependency needs   ___Timing and maturity level

Your current age:

_____

The age you feel:

_____

Are you registered to vote?
     [   ]yes [   ]no
           Do you know how to spot a poisonous snake?
                  [   ]yes [   ]no

Which of the seven deadly sins are you
most guilty of committing?
___Envy   ___Pride
___Gluttony   ___Sloth
___Greed   ___Wrath
___Lust

Have you donated something to charity?
     [   ]yes [   ]no
           Have you participated in community service?
                  [   ]yes [   ]no
Have you given money to a homeless person?
     [   ]yes [   ]no

You're most like which one of the following types of people:
___I forgive and forget
___I hold a grudge
___I get even
___I don't take things too personally to begin with

When Someone Says, You Think...

Cardboard

_____

Cards

_____

Carwashes

_____

Castles

_____

Caves

_____

Cemeteries

_____

Chalk

_____

Chaos

_____

Chapstick

_____

Chlorine

_____

Cigarettes

_____

Circles

_____

Clocks

_____

Closets

_____

Clouds

_____

Cookies

_____

When Someone Says, You Think...

Cops

_____

Corduroy

_____

Cramps

_____

Crayons

_____

Crucifixes

_____

Cubes

_____

Death

_____

Deceit

_____

Dirt

_____

Drums

_____

Eggs

_____

Elevators

_____

Envelopes

_____

Exhaust

_____

Fans

_____

Fat

_____

Ethics and Morality

Have you ever thought a murderer had an excusable motive
to kill another human being?

    [   ]yes [   ]no

Have you ever thought a murderer's view of the world
was somehow better than yours?

    [   ]yes [   ]no

Have you ever threatened to kill someone?

    [   ]yes [   ]no

Have you ever killed an animal?

    [   ]yes [   ]no

Have you ever made a racist remark?

    [   ]yes [   ]no

Do you believe in life after death?

    [   ]yes [   ]no

What are you really thinking when someone of a religion
other than your own tries to preach to you?

_____

_____

Have you laughed at someone with a mental handicap?

    [   ]yes [   ]no

Would you date someone with a mental handicap?

    [   ]yes [   ]no

Have you cheated on someone?

    [   ]yes [   ]no

Have you made fun of a friend behind their back?

    [   ]yes [   ]no

Do you believe life begins at the moment of conception?

    [   ]yes [   ]no

Would you steal to prevent a murder?

    [   ]yes [   ]no

Should we condone assisted suicide for the terminally ill?

    [   ]yes [   ]no

Would you rape to ensure the survival of our species?

    [   ]yes [   ]no

At Random

What do you like to do on your birthday?

_____

_____

Are you normally attracted to people who are older or younger?

_____

Describe the greatest kiss of your life:

_____

_____

Do you have a famous relative?
    [   ]yes [   ]no
                    Do plain white walls freak you out?
                        [   ]yes [   ]no
Do you clean toilet seats before sitting on them?
    [   ]yes [   ]no
 Did you ever pretend to be sick so you didn't have to go to school?
                        [   ]yes [   ]no
Do you cuss freely outside of mixed company?
    [   ]yes [   ]no
                    Can you take a bra off with one hand?
                        [   ]yes [   ]no

If you had to say hell was somewhere on Earth, where would you claim it to be?

_____

If you could convince every person on the planet of something, it would be what?

_____

_____

The name of the best cook you know:

_____

Your Lists

Reasons you've spoken to the police:

1.)_____
2.)_____
3.)_____
4.)_____
5.)_____
6.)_____
7.)_____
8.)_____
9.)_____
10.)_____

Reasons you've visited a hospital:

1.)_____
2.)_____
3.)_____
4.)_____
5.)_____
6.)_____
7.)_____
8.)_____
9.)_____
10.)_____

Your Lists

Things you'd do as a mad scientist:

1.)_____
2.)_____
3.)_____
4.)_____
5.)_____
6.)_____
7.)_____
8.)_____
9.)_____
10.)_____

Things you wish didn't exist:

1.)_____
2.)_____
3.)_____
4.)_____
5.)_____
6.)_____
7.)_____
8.)_____
9.)_____
10.)_____

At Random

Do you believe all crop circles are manmade?
    [   ]yes [   ]no

                        Do you believe vampires exist?
                                    [   ]yes [   ]no

Do you believe aliens had anything to do
with the creation of Stonehenge?
    [   ]yes [   ]no

                  Do you believe the Holy Grail ever existed?
                                    [   ]yes [   ]no

Do you believe zombies are possible?
    [   ]yes [   ]no

                          Do you believe Bigfoot exists?
                                    [   ]yes [   ]no

Do you believe in the power of curses?
    [   ]yes [   ]no

                  Do you believe perpetual motion is possible?
                                    [   ]yes [   ]no

Do you believe aliens had anything to do with the statues
found on Easter Island?
    [   ]yes [   ]no

                  Do you believe the Loch Ness Monster exists?
                                    [   ]yes [   ]no

Do you believe that your personality traits
are determined by your birthday?
    [   ]yes [   ]no

                          Do you believe in voodoo?
                                    [   ]yes [   ]no

Do you believe in reincarnation?
    [   ]yes [   ]no

            Do you believe that slaves built the Egyptian pyramids?
                                    [   ]yes [   ]no

Do you believe the Chupacabra exists?
    [   ]yes [   ]no

                  Do you believe that your personality traits
                      are determined by your facial features?
                                    [   ]yes [   ]no

At Random

Have you dined alone at a restaurant?
[   ]yes [   ]no

Have you eaten raw meat?
[   ]yes [   ]no

Have you kept a journal or diary?
[   ]yes [   ]no

Have you called the cops on someone for any reason?
[   ]yes [   ]no

Have you been in a car accident?
[   ]yes [   ]no

Have you lived alone?
[   ]yes [   ]no

Have you been stung by a bee?
[   ]yes [   ]no

Have you been stalked?
[   ]yes [   ]no

Have you been to a concert?
[   ]yes [   ]no

Have you been handcuffed for any reason?
[   ]yes [   ]no

Have you witnessed a death?
[   ]yes [   ]no

Have you purchased something at a thrift store?
[   ]yes [   ]no

Have you been to a professional sporting event?
[   ]yes [   ]no

Have you completed your income taxes by yourself?
[   ]yes [   ]no

Have you shot a gun at someone?
[   ]yes [   ]no

Have you been shot at?
[   ]yes [   ]no

Have you swum in a pool during a thunderstorm?
[   ]yes [   ]no

Have you dressed up like the opposite sex?
[   ]yes [   ]no

Your Lists

Jobs you wouldn't want to have:

1.)_____

2.)_____

3.)_____

4.)_____

5.)_____

6.)_____

7.)_____

8.)_____

9.)_____

10.)_____

Jobs you'd like to try:

1.)_____

2.)_____

3.)_____

4.)_____

5.)_____

6.)_____

7.)_____

8.)_____

9.)_____

10.)_____

Your Lists

Animals you're afraid of:

1.)_____
2.)_____
3.)_____
4.)_____
5.)_____
6.)_____
7.)_____
8.)_____
9.)_____
10.)_____

Bands you've seen live:

1.)_____
2.)_____
3.)_____
4.)_____
5.)_____
6.)_____
7.)_____
8.)_____
9.)_____
10.)_____

Superstitions

Do you believe it's bad luck to kill a spider?
  [ ]yes [ ]no
    Do you believe someone born on Halloween will have
      the ability to communicate with the dead?
            [ ]yes [ ]no
Would you take advice from a magic 8 ball?
  [ ]yes [ ]no
   Do you believe it's unlucky if two people say the same word
     at the same time and don't immediately call it a jinx?
            [ ]yes [ ]no
Do you believe it's unlucky to meet under mistletoe
and not kiss the person?
  [ ]yes [ ]no
    Do you believe it's unlucky to see your face in a mirror
            by candlelight?
            [ ]yes [ ]no
Do you believe it's unlucky to send Christmas carolers
away empty-handed?
  [ ]yes [ ]no
    Do you believe it's unlucky to walk under a ladder?
            [ ]yes [ ]no
Do you believe lightning will never strike a home
in which the fireplace is lit?
  [ ]yes [ ]no
    Do you believe people who hiccup are momentarily
        possessed by the devil?
            [ ]yes [ ]no
Do you believe salty soup is a sign that the cook is in love?
  [ ]yes [ ]no
  Do you believe sneezing with your head turned to the left or right
      determines the fortune in your near future?
            [ ]yes [ ]no
Do you believe some people act crazier than they otherwise would
when the moon is full?
  [ ]yes [ ]no
        Do you believe storks deliver babies?
            [ ]yes [ ]no

Your Least Favorites

Accent:

_____

Branch of science:

_____

Bridge:

_____

Card game:

_____

Cat breed:

_____

Clothing material:

_____

Constellation:

_____

Dog breed:

_____

Emotion:

_____

Gemstone:

_____

Government program:

_____

Insect:

_____

Instrument:

_____

Olympic event:

_____

Religion:

_____

Spice:

_____

Technological device:

_____

Type of weather:

_____

Your Lists

Nicknames of yours which you hate:

1.)_____
2.)_____
3.)_____
4.)_____
5.)_____
6.)_____
7.)_____
8.)_____
9.)_____
10.)_____

Things which make you nervous:

1.)_____
2.)_____
3.)_____
4.)_____
5.)_____
6.)_____
7.)_____
8.)_____
9.)_____
10.)_____

Your Lists

Kind things you've done for strangers:

1.)_____
2.)_____
3.)_____
4.)_____
5.)_____
6.)_____
7.)_____
8.)_____
9.)_____
10.)_____

People you regret hurting:

1.)_____
2.)_____
3.)_____
4.)_____
5.)_____
6.)_____
7.)_____
8.)_____
9.)_____
10.)_____

At Random

How many times have you been cheated on?

_____

Your thoughts on open relationships:

_____

Have you broken up with someone so that you
could date someone else?

     [   ]yes [   ]no

                  Do you think you're likeable?

                      [   ]yes [   ]no

Do you enjoy meeting new people?

     [   ]yes [   ]no

                  Do you think you're a good kisser?

                      [   ]yes [   ]no

Do you think there are people you haven't seen since your youth
who still think about you from time to time?

     [   ]yes [   ]no

                  Do you make friends easily?

                      [   ]yes [   ]no

Do you dwell too long on others' opinions of you?

     [   ]yes [   ]no

          Have you maintained a friendship with any of your exes?

                      [   ]yes [   ]no

Do you ever find yourself attracted to people whose personalities
you loathe?

     [   ]yes [   ]no

                  Have you kissed a member of the same sex?

                      [   ]yes [   ]no

Someone you flirt with on a regular basis:

_____

How many times have you been dumped?

_____

At Random

Do you believe ghosts exist?

    [   ]yes [   ]no

            Do you believe your personality traits
are determined by your name?

            [   ]yes [   ]no

Do you flirt with people you'd never date?

    [   ]yes [   ]no

            Do you believe people can change their own nature?

            [   ]yes [   ]no

Do you think that your belief about what happens
when we die could be wrong?

    [   ]yes [   ]no

            Do you believe something strange is at work
in the Bermuda Triangle?

            [   ]yes [   ]no

Do you believe in demonic possession?

    [   ]yes [   ]no

            Do you believe poltergeists exist?

            [   ]yes [   ]no

Do you believe in numerology?

    [   ]yes [   ]no

            Do you believe Stigmata is a real condition?

            [   ]yes [   ]no

Do you believe Spontaneous Human Combustion is factual?

    [   ]yes [   ]no

            Do you believe crystals have magical properties?

            [   ]yes [   ]no

Do you believe in the Big Bang Theory?

    [   ]yes [   ]no

            Do you believe the Yeti exists?

            [   ]yes [   ]no

Do you believe aliens had anything to do with the creation
of the Nazca Lines?

    [   ]yes [   ]no

            Do you believe in palmistry?

            [   ]yes [   ]no

Your Lists

The most painful things you've endured:

1.)_____
2.)_____
3.)_____
4.)_____
5.)_____
6.)_____
7.)_____
8.)_____
9.)_____
10.)_____

Causes you'd support:

1.)_____
2.)_____
3.)_____
4.)_____
5.)_____
6.)_____
7.)_____
8.)_____
9.)_____
10.)_____

Your Lists

The greatest bumper stickers you've seen:

1.)_____
2.)_____
3.)_____
4.)_____
5.)_____
6.)_____
7.)_____
8.)_____
9.)_____
10.)_____

Basic tenets of your political views:

1.)_____
2.)_____
3.)_____
4.)_____
5.)_____
6.)_____
7.)_____
8.)_____
9.)_____
10.)_____

Your Views On Conspiracy Theories

The moon landing was faked.
    [   ]true [   ]false

A secret group of people are in line with an alien race
in an attempt to take over the world.
    [   ]true [   ]false

The CIA peddles drugs worldwide.
    [   ]true [   ]false

The Sphinx is actually much older than the pyramids of Giza.
    [   ]true [   ]false

A US government facility in the arctic is performing top secret
experiments dealing with weather control, and the like.
    [   ]true [   ]false

JFK was not assassinated by Lee Harvey Oswald.
    [   ]true [   ]false

There is or was life on Mars.
    [   ]true [   ]false

The Rendlesham UFO encounter was genuine.
    [   ]true [   ]false

Global warming is not a real phenomenon.
    [   ]true [   ]false

Our brains are capable of doing things far beyond
what we've been led to believe.
    [   ]true [   ]false

Cattle mutilation is an alien oriented phenomenon.
    [   ]true [   ]false

TWA Flight 800 was blown up by a US Navy missile.
    [   ]true [   ]false

Tupac Shakur faked his own death.
    [   ]true [   ]false

The Mothman was an escaped government experiment.
    [   ]true [   ]false

Your Views On Conspiracy Theories

The moon is a hollow alien base disguised
as a natural satellite.

[   ]true [   ]false

The government has experimented successfully with time travel.

[   ]true [   ]false

Elvis is still alive.

[   ]true [   ]false

The Men In Black are actually aliens cleverly disguised
as humans.

[   ]true [   ]false

There's a code in the bible indicating it to be
the handiwork of God.

[   ]true [   ]false

We were genetically altered sometime in the distant past by
an alien race.

[   ]true [   ]false

Our government is reverse-engineering
alien technology at Area 51.

[   ]true [   ]false

What crashed in Roswell was not a weather balloon,
but an alien spacecraft.

[   ]true [   ]false

Marilyn Monroe was murdered.

[   ]true [   ]false

Our government is using psychics to spy on US citizens.

[   ]true [   ]false

An alien race exists within our oceans and are
covertly controlling the planet.

[   ]true [   ]false

Martin Luther King was not assassinated by James Earl Ray.

[   ]true [   ]false

When Someone Says, You Think...

Feathers

_____

Fever

_____

Fireplaces

_____

Flags

_____

Flannel

_____

Flashlights

_____

Fleece

_____

Flour

_____

Fog

_____

Fossils

_____

Garlic

_____

Gas

_____

Gravity

_____

Gravy

_____

Guitars

_____

Guns

_____

When Someone Says, You Think...

Hail

_____

Hammers

_____

Hammocks

_____

Handicaps

_____

Handshakes

_____

Hangovers

_____

Headphones

_____

Highways

_____

Holes

_____

Honeysuckle

_____

Hugs

_____

Hunger

_____

Icicles

_____

Infections

_____

Ink

_____

Insanity

_____

At Random

If you had to work at a fast food restaurant, which would it be?

_____

If you suddenly found yourself living in the age of the dinosaurs, you'd survive by doing what?

_____

_____

If you were a lawyer, what sort of people would you want to help?

_____

If you were to host or star in a television show, which would it be?

_____

If you discovered that your best friend and your significant other were secretly seeing each other, who would you be angrier with?

_____

If you could get away with any crime, what would it be?

_____

If you had to go streaking, you'd do it where?

_____

If time travel were possible, would you visit the future or the past?

_____

If you could be a member of a race other than your own, it would be which race?

_____

If you were homeless, your cardboard sign would read:

_____

At Random

What do you wear to bed?

_____

The name of your favorite soap:

_____

The name of your favorite shampoo:

_____

You prefer to wear which of the following most often:
___Boxers   ___Thongs
___Briefs   ___No underwear at all
___Panties

How often do you brush your teeth?

_____

The name of your favorite toothpaste:

_____

Have you used a toothbrush which wasn't your own?
    [   ]yes [   ]no
    Have you gone a week or more without bathing or showering?
                                    [   ]yes [   ]no

How many times per day do you usually eat?

_____

Have you gone a whole day without eating?
    [   ]yes [   ]no

How many hours of sleep would you say you average per night?

_____

Your Lists

Great ways to break the ice with strangers:

1.)_____
2.)_____
3.)_____
4.)_____
5.)_____
6.)_____
7.)_____
8.)_____
9.)_____
10.)_____

Your pet peeves:

1.)_____
2.)_____
3.)_____
4.)_____
5.)_____
6.)_____
7.)_____
8.)_____
9.)_____
10.)_____

Your Lists

Your guilty pleasures:

1.)_____

2.)_____

3.)_____

4.)_____

5.)_____

6.)_____

7.)_____

8.)_____

9.)_____

10.)_____

The world needs more:

1.)_____

2.)_____

3.)_____

4.)_____

5.)_____

6.)_____

7.)_____

8.)_____

9.)_____

10.)_____

At Random

What would you like to find in your mailbox?

_____

Do your friends tend to be mostly males or females?

_____

Have you named a part of your body?
    [   ]yes [   ]no

If that was a yes, what part was it and what did you name it?

_____

What do you think happens when we die?

_____

_____

If you lost all memory of your life, would you
keep living the life you live now?
[   ]yes [   ]no

What is your favorite kind of apple?

_____

If you could change one thing about human nature,
what would it be?

_____

How many pairs of shoes do you own?

_____

What constitutes a serious relationship?

_____

_____

At Random

Do you pluck your eyebrows?

[   ]yes [   ]no

As a magician, you'd pull what out of your hat?

_____

Have you been bitten by a spider or snake?

[   ]yes [   ]no

Have you bet money on something?

[   ]yes [   ]no

How do you get rid of hiccups?

_____

Have you tasted mineral water?

[   ]yes [   ]no

Have you had surgery?

[   ]yes [   ]no

Your longest relationship lasted:

_____

Have you made fire without the help of a lighter,
a match, or any form of electricity?

[   ]yes [   ]no

Have you gone more than a week without using a phone?

[   ]yes [   ]no

How long can you hold your breath underwater?

_____

Has anyone given you flowers?

[   ]yes [   ]no

Have you made your own beer or wine?

[   ]yes [   ]no

Your Lists

Things you should never tell someone:

1.)_____
2.)_____
3.)_____
4.)_____
5.)_____
6.)_____
7.)_____
8.)_____
9.)_____
10.)_____

Pets you'd enjoy having:

1.)_____
2.)_____
3.)_____
4.)_____
5.)_____
6.)_____
7.)_____
8.)_____
9.)_____
10.)_____

Your Lists

Reasons to end a relationship:

1.)_____
2.)_____
3.)_____
4.)_____
5.)_____
6.)_____
7.)_____
8.)_____
9.)_____
10.)_____

Things you miss about being a child:

1.)_____
2.)_____
3.)_____
4.)_____
5.)_____
6.)_____
7.)_____
8.)_____
9.)_____
10.)_____

THIS or THAT

Love	___OR___	Money
Top bunk	___OR___	Bottom bunk
Chocolate	___OR___	Vanilla
Pool	___OR___	Hot tub
Die drowning	___OR___	Die burning
High maintenance	___OR___	Low maintenance
Deaf	___OR___	Blind
Coffee	___OR___	Tea
Stoplights	___OR___	Heavy traffic
Hugs	___OR___	Kisses
Sunrise	___OR___	Sunset
Taking pictures	___OR___	Being in pictures
Democrat	___OR___	Republican
Introvert	___OR___	Extrovert
Paper	___OR___	Plastic
Caffeine	___OR___	Sugar
Lake	___OR___	Ocean
Obese	___OR___	Anorexic
Morning shower	___OR___	Evening shower
Right handed	___OR___	Left handed
Campsites	___OR___	Hotels
Gold	___OR___	Silver
Day	___OR___	Night
Car	___OR___	Truck
Moon	___OR___	Stars
Travel	___OR___	Rest
Friday nights	___OR___	Sunday mornings
Hot dog	___OR___	Hamburger
Homeless	___OR___	Carless
Romance	___OR___	Honesty
Give	___OR___	Take
A cleaning robot	___OR___	A cooking robot

THIS or THAT

Roller skates	___OR___	Rollerblades
Music	___OR___	Photography
Duct tape	___OR___	Scotch tape
Alzheimer's disease	___OR___	Parkinson's disease
Teddy bears	___OR___	Dolls
Mystery	___OR___	Understanding
Diet	___OR___	Exercise
Overly cocky	___OR___	Overly insecure
Baby powder	___OR___	Baby oil
Caribbean cruise	___OR___	Arctic cruise
Cuddling	___OR___	Holding hands
Dentist visit	___OR___	Doctor visit
Table games	___OR___	Video games
Cotton candy	___OR___	Funnel cake
Volleyball	___OR___	Frisbee
Bottle	___OR___	Can
Gift wrap	___OR___	Gift bag
Dice	___OR___	Dominoes
Fix it yourself	___OR___	Pay someone to fix it
Drive	___OR___	Fly
Sarcasm	___OR___	Seriousness
Take a shower	___OR___	Take a bath
Zoos	___OR___	Aquariums
Same sex twins	___OR___	Differing sex twins
Public libraries	___OR___	Public parks
Cardio	___OR___	Weight training
Books	___OR___	Movies
Tennis shoes	___OR___	Flip flops
Carpet	___OR___	Tile
Flowers	___OR___	Candy
Adventure	___OR___	Comfort
Staples	___OR___	Paperclips

Your Lists

Things you'd do if you were invisible:

1.)_____
2.)_____
3.)_____
4.)_____
5.)_____
6.)_____
7.)_____
8.)_____
9.)_____
10.)_____

Past civilizations you're interested in:

1.)_____
2.)_____
3.)_____
4.)_____
5.)_____
6.)_____
7.)_____
8.)_____
9.)_____
10.)_____

Your Lists

Questions you'd like answers to:

1.)_____
2.)_____
3.)_____
4.)_____
5.)_____
6.)_____
7.)_____
8.)_____
9.)_____
10.)_____

Rules you live your life by:

1.)_____
2.)_____
3.)_____
4.)_____
5.)_____
6.)_____
7.)_____
8.)_____
9.)_____
10.)_____

Which Would You Prefer?

The human population suddenly cut in half
___OR___
The human population suddenly doubled

Dying hated for a life of honesty
___OR___
Dying loved for a life of lies

The upper class losing 50% of their income to taxation
___OR___
The lower class losing 50% of their income to taxation

Gay marriage being legal
___OR___
Polygamy being legal

A rapist going unpunished
___OR___
A murderer going unpunished

Unregulated animal testing and stem cell research
___OR___
Never finding cures for cancer and AIDS

A possibly innocent man put to death
___OR___
A possibly guilty murderer set free

Necrophilia legalized
___OR___
Bestiality legalized

The loss of the historical record
___OR___
The scientific method being outlawed

Which Would You Prefer?

The sexual abuse of a child
___OR___
The aborting of a fetus

The eradication of the bible
___OR___
The eradication of the US Constitution

The extinction of dogs
___OR___
The slaughter of two billion random humans

Marijuana being legal
___OR___
Alcohol being illegal

Science taught in Christian churches
___OR___
The tenets of Islam taught in public schools

The murdering of a toddler
___OR___
The murdering of an elderly person

Losing an arm
___OR___
Having a child born with a severe mental handicap

Children allowed to carry firearms in public schools
___OR___
The legalization of all narcotics

No punishment for a spouse physically abusing their partner
___OR___
No punishment for a parent mentally abusing their child

Your Lists

Things you worry about:

1.)_____

2.)_____

3.)_____

4.)_____

5.)_____

6.)_____

7.)_____

8.)_____

9.)_____

10.)_____

Things you're obsessed with:

1.)_____

2.)_____

3.)_____

4.)_____

5.)_____

6.)_____

7.)_____

8.)_____

9.)_____

10.)_____

Your Lists

Things you're allergic to:

1.)_____
2.)_____
3.)_____
4.)_____
5.)_____
6.)_____
7.)_____
8.)_____
9.)_____
10.)_____

Things which aren't worth learning:

1.)_____
2.)_____
3.)_____
4.)_____
5.)_____
6.)_____
7.)_____
8.)_____
9.)_____
10.)_____

At Random

Have you driven a vehicle with a manual transmission?
    [   ]yes [   ]no

                                       Have you had stitches?
                                       [   ]yes [   ]no

Have you seen the Aurora Borealis with your own eyes?
    [   ]yes [   ]no

                                       Have you ridden in a taxi?
                                       [   ]yes [   ]no

Have you been fired from a job?
    [   ]yes [   ]no

                                       Have you had Chicken Pox?
                                       [   ]yes [   ]no

Have you been on a blind date?
    [   ]yes [   ]no

                                     Have you taken part in a protest?
                                       [   ]yes [   ]no

Have you signed a petition?
    [   ]yes [   ]no

                           Have you placed an ad in your local newspaper?
                                       [   ]yes [   ]no

Have you cut someone's hair?
    [   ]yes [   ]no

                                     Have you performed on a stage?
                                       [   ]yes [   ]no

Have you had an allergic reaction?
    [   ]yes [   ]no

                                     Have you contemplated suicide?
                                       [   ]yes [   ]no

Have you made a prank call?
    [   ]yes [   ]no

                                     Have you broken a bone?
                                       [   ]yes [   ]no

Have you been hunting?
    [   ]yes [   ]no

                         Have you used jumper cables to start a car battery?
                                       [   ]yes [   ]no

At Random

Have you licked a 9 volt battery?

[   ]yes [   ]no

Have you had a close friend confess their love for you?

[   ]yes [   ]no

Have you been stranded with no money, no phone
and no working vehicle?

[   ]yes [   ]no

Have you purchased something online?

[   ]yes [   ]no

Do you consider yourself a spiritual person?

[   ]yes [   ]no

Have you been so intoxicated that you woke up
not knowing what you'd done the night before?

[   ]yes [   ]no

Have you peed in a swimming pool?

[   ]yes [   ]no

Have you practiced kissing on your hand or arm?

[   ]yes [   ]no

Have you sniffed an article of clothing which did not
belong to you?

[   ]yes [   ]no

Have you purposely caused a couple to break up?

[   ]yes [   ]no

Have you forced yourself to puke?

[   ]yes [   ]no

Have you slept naked?

[   ]yes [   ]no

Have you stuck chewed gum under a chair?

[   ]yes [   ]no

Have you danced like no one was watching?

[   ]yes [   ]no

Have you buried some sort of memorabilia in hopes someone
will discover it in the future?

[   ]yes [   ]no

Have you used a tanning bed?

[   ]yes [   ]no

Your Lists

Ways to lure you into a trap:

1.)_____
2.)_____
3.)_____
4.)_____
5.)_____
6.)_____
7.)_____
8.)_____
9.)_____
10.)_____

Ways you wouldn't want to die:

1.)_____
2.)_____
3.)_____
4.)_____
5.)_____
6.)_____
7.)_____
8.)_____
9.)_____
10.)_____

Your Lists

Fictional creatures you wish were real:

1.)_____
2.)_____
3.)_____
4.)_____
5.)_____
6.)_____
7.)_____
8.)_____
9.)_____
10.)_____

Ways you'd prefer to die:

1.)_____
2.)_____
3.)_____
4.)_____
5.)_____
6.)_____
7.)_____
8.)_____
9.)_____
10.)_____

At Random

Have you been punched in the face?
[   ]yes [   ]no

Have you poured salt on a snail?
[   ]yes [   ]no

How many different homes have you lived in?

_____

How many vehicles have you owned?

_____

Have you lied about dating someone?
[   ]yes [   ]no

Have you lied about your age?
[   ]yes [   ]no

If you had to have plastic surgery, what would you have done?

_____

How old were you when you last Trick 'r Treated?

_____

Is a prenuptial agreement important to you when considering marriage?
[   ]yes [   ]no

Did you attend your high school prom?
[   ]yes [   ]no

How do you behave when you're nervous?

_____

_____

If you were an alien, you would visit the Earth for what reason?

_____

At Random

If you lost all memory of your life, who would you be glad
you couldn't remember?

_____

Have you run over an animal while driving?
    [   ]yes [   ]no
            Have you heard of a blind person reporting a haunting?
                                [   ]yes [   ]no

If you were going to place a video camera in your own home,
in which room would you place it?

_____

You tend to sleep mostly on:
___Your back   ___Your right side
___Your left side   ___Your stomach

The most money you've ever bet on something:

_____

Have you stayed awake for more than 48 hours straight?
    [   ]yes [   ]no
                  Have you fallen asleep at work?
                              [   ]yes [   ]no

If you could relive one moment of your life,
which moment would you choose?

_____

_____

If you had an identical twin, would you ever trade places for fun?
    [   ]yes [   ]no
            Are you still close to any of your grade school friends?
                                [   ]yes [   ]no

When Someone Says, You Think...

Iron

_____

Kites

_____

Lakes

_____

Laughter

_____

Lightning

_____

Lipstick

_____

Locks

_____

Lotion

_____

Love

_____

Magic

_____

Magnets

_____

Mailboxes

_____

Manholes

_____

Marshmallows

_____

Midgets

_____

Milk

_____

When Someone Says, You Think...

Moonlight

_____

Motorcycles

_____

Mountains

_____

Mud

_____

Nails

_____

Ninjas

_____

Oceans

_____

Ornaments

_____

Paperclips

_____

Parachutes

_____

Pencils

_____

Peppermints

_____

Pianos

_____

Picnics

_____

Plains

_____

Pools

_____

The Criminal In You

Did you smoke tobacco under the age of 18?
[   ]yes [   ]no

Have you fished without a license?
[   ]yes [   ]no

Have you taken something from work without paying for it?
[   ]yes [   ]no

Have you trespassed on private property?
[   ]yes [   ]no

Have you opened mail which wasn't yours?
[   ]yes [   ]no

Have you taken an illegal drug?
[   ]yes [   ]no

Have you stolen anything from a significant other?
[   ]yes [   ]no

If that was a yes, then what did you steal?

_____

Have you been arrested?
[   ]yes [   ]no

Have you driven under the influence of a mind-altering substance?
[   ]yes [   ]no

Have you been to court?
[   ]yes [   ]no

Have you stalked someone?
[   ]yes [   ]no

Have you vandalized someone else's property?
[   ]yes [   ]no

Have you been intoxicated at work?
[   ]yes [   ]no

Have you sold anything illegal?
[   ]yes [   ]no

Has anyone called the cops on you?
[   ]yes [   ]no

The Criminal In You

Have you lied to the cops?
[   ]yes [   ]no

Have you run from the cops?
[   ]yes [   ]no

Have you driven without car insurance?
[   ]yes [   ]no

Have you run a red light?
[   ]yes [   ]no

Have you ridden in a car without wearing a seatbelt?
[   ]yes [   ]no

Have you driven a vehicle with an outdated
registration or inspection sticker?
[   ]yes [   ]no

Have you passed another vehicle in a 'no passing' zone?
[   ]yes [   ]no

Have you driven someone else's vehicle without their permission?
[   ]yes [   ]no

Have you copied something from a book or online source
and claimed it was your own work?
[   ]yes [   ]no

Have you stolen money from your parents?
[   ]yes [   ]no

Have you skipped school?
[   ]yes [   ]no

Have you toilet papered someone's home?
[   ]yes [   ]no

Have you slashed someone's tires?
[   ]yes [   ]no

Have you stolen a street sign?
[   ]yes [   ]no

Have you been searched by the cops?
[   ]yes [   ]no

Have you bought alcohol or tobacco for a minor?
[   ]yes [   ]no

Your Lists

Some of your greatest fears:

1.)_____
2.)_____
3.)_____
4.)_____
5.)_____
6.)_____
7.)_____
8.)_____
9.)_____
10.)_____

People you'd kill if you could get away with it:

1.)_____
2.)_____
3.)_____
4.)_____
5.)_____
6.)_____
7.)_____
8.)_____
9.)_____
10.)_____

Your Lists

Songs which make you want to dance:

1.)_____

2.)_____

3.)_____

4.)_____

5.)_____

6.)_____

7.)_____

8.)_____

9.)_____

10.)_____

Events you'd want to witness as a traveler in time:

1.)_____

2.)_____

3.)_____

4.)_____

5.)_____

6.)_____

7.)_____

8.)_____

9.)_____

10.)_____

Which Would You Prefer?

A jobless child who never leaves home
___OR___
A successful child who moves halfway around the world

Marrying someone who has multiple children with multiple people
___OR___
Marrying someone who can never have children

A government which doesn't allow citizens to become billionaires
___OR___
A government which allows the poorest citizens to starve

The burning of American flags
___OR___
The burning of Christian bibles

A sexually active teen who was taught safe sex in school
___OR___
A sexually active teen who wasn't

Having to live with no right to privacy
___OR___
Having to live with an increased risk of terrorism

A god which insists upon eternal torture
___OR___
No god at all

A world with no right to carry firearms
___OR___
A world with no space program

Businesses controlling government
___OR___
Government controlling businesses

Which Would You Prefer?

Prostitution legalized in all states; regulated for safety
___OR___
Prostitution made illegal in all states; punishable by imprisonment

Lower gas prices
___OR___
Better environmental protections

Searching for life on other worlds
___OR___
Colonizing the moon

Taking a very sick child to a hospital, without prayer
___OR___
Keeping a very sick child at home, praying for miraculous healing

A partner who openly engages in sex with other people
___OR___
A partner who has no interest in sex

The inability to travel outside of the US
___OR___
Citizenship for all illegal immigrants

Believing comforting things which are very likely untrue
___OR___
Believing discomforting things which are very likely true

A child who grows up and partners with a life-like doll
___OR___
A child who grows up and partners with a family member

An endless and free supply of food and clean water for all humans
___OR___
The ability to live twice as long with the aging process cut in half

Your Lists

People you think would make great presidents:

1.)_____

2.)_____

3.)_____

4.)_____

5.)_____

6.)_____

7.)_____

8.)_____

9.)_____

10.)_____

People you've known who have died:

1.)_____

2.)_____

3.)_____

4.)_____

5.)_____

6.)_____

7.)_____

8.)_____

9.)_____

10.)_____

Your Lists

People you'd love to see a bird poop on:

1.)_____
2.)_____
3.)_____
4.)_____
5.)_____
6.)_____
7.)_____
8.)_____
9.)_____
10.)_____

People who give the best hugs:

1.)_____
2.)_____
3.)_____
4.)_____
5.)_____
6.)_____
7.)_____
8.)_____
9.)_____
10.)_____

Superstitions

Do you believe that if someone gives you a pocket knife
already open that you must give it back in the same manner?
[   ]yes [   ]no
    Do you believe that if you catch a falling leaf on the first day
of autumn that you won't come down with a cold all winter?
[   ]yes [   ]no

Would you take advice from a Ouija board?
[   ]yes [   ]no
    Do you believe that if you see rats leaving a ship,
it means the ship is going to sink?
[   ]yes [   ]no

Do you believe that if you sing before 7 you'll cry before 11?
[   ]yes [   ]no
    Do you believe empty pockets on New Year's day
signals a year of poverty?
[   ]yes [   ]no

Do you believe that if you touch a loved one who has died
you won't have dreams about them?
[   ]yes [   ]no
    Do you believe that pulling out a gray hair will cause
ten more to grow in its place?
[   ]yes [   ]no

Do you believe that seeing a lone fox is lucky?
[   ]yes [   ]no
    Would you be afraid to camp out in a cemetery for a night?
[   ]yes [   ]no

Do you believe that someone who cuts bread in an uneven manner
has recently been lying?
[   ]yes [   ]no
Do you believe that hanging wind chimes in or around your home
will keep evil spirits at bay?
[   ]yes [   ]no

Would you feel uneasy if you saw an owl during the daylight?
[   ]yes [   ]no
    Do you believe touching a frog will mean infertility?
[   ]yes [   ]no

Your Favorites

Accent:

_____

Branch of science:

_____

Bridge:

_____

Card game:

_____

Cat breed:

_____

Clothing material:

_____

Constellation:

_____

Dog breed:

_____

Emotion:

_____

Gemstone:

_____

Government program:

_____

Insect:

_____

Instrument:

_____

Olympic event:

_____

Religion:

_____

Spice:

_____

Technological device:

_____

Type of weather:

_____

Your Lists

Names you'd give a child:

1.)_____
2.)_____
3.)_____
4.)_____
5.)_____
6.)_____
7.)_____
8.)_____
9.)_____
10.)_____

The world's most worthless inventions:

1.)_____
2.)_____
3.)_____
4.)_____
5.)_____
6.)_____
7.)_____
8.)_____
9.)_____
10.)_____

Your Lists

Languages you'd love to be able to speak:

1.)_____
2.)_____
3.)_____
4.)_____
5.)_____
6.)_____
7.)_____
8.)_____
9.)_____
10.)_____

Things your family taught you to appreciate:

1.)_____
2.)_____
3.)_____
4.)_____
5.)_____
6.)_____
7.)_____
8.)_____
9.)_____
10.)_____

At Random

Things you've been known to do in your sleep:

___Drool   ___Sing
___Hit   ___Sleepwalk
___Kick   ___Smack
___Open your eyes   ___Snore
___Scream   ___Talk

You'd rather see which one of the following species go extinct:

___Cats   ___Elephants
___Chickens   ___Horses
___Cows   ___Pigs
___Dogs   ___Squirrels
___Dolphins   ___Whales

Types of homes you've lived in:

___Apartment   ___Igloo
___Boat   ___Loft
___Cabin   ___Mobile home
___Car   ___RV
___Condominium   ___Teepee
___Duplex   ___Tent
___House   ___Townhome

You have the biggest issues with which one of the following:

___Allergies   ___Headaches
___Constipation   ___Indigestion
___Diarrhea   ___Muscle aches
___Gas   ___Rashes

Forms of punishment you received as a child:

___Bedroom confinement   ___Mouth washed out with soap
___Boxed ears   ___Paddling
___Grounding   ___Spanking
___Lashing   ___Time out
___Made to stand in the corner

At Random

Art forms you've tried your hand at:

___Acting	___Painting
___Architecture	___Photography
___Crafts	___Sculpting
___Culinary	___Sewing
___Dance	___Singing
___Drawing	___Video
___Landscaping	___Woodworking
___Music	___Writing

Would you rather sleep alone or with someone else in the bed?

_____

Something you like to make fun of:

_____

Which natural resource do you think we'll run out of first:

___Coal	___Petroleum
___Natural gas	___Timber
___Oil	___Water

What mythical creature would you be, were it possible?

_____

Something you've purposely hidden from your parents:

_____

Reasons you would watch the news:

___A particular newscaster	___Positive messages
___Celebrity gossip	___Stock market specifics
___Consumer alerts	___Strange crimes
___Crazy stories	___The weather forecast
___Deaths	___Traffic reports
___Political updates	___World events

Your Lists

The strangest things you've placed on a to-do list:

1.)_____

2.)_____

3.)_____

4.)_____

5.)_____

6.)_____

7.)_____

8.)_____

9.)_____

10.)_____

The celebrities you've been in closest proximity to:

1.)_____

2.)_____

3.)_____

4.)_____

5.)_____

6.)_____

7.)_____

8.)_____

9.)_____

10.)_____

Your Lists

Some of your school teachers' names:

1.)_____

2.)_____

3.)_____

4.)_____

5.)_____

6.)_____

7.)_____

8.)_____

9.)_____

10.)_____

Things you don't miss about being a child:

1.)_____

2.)_____

3.)_____

4.)_____

5.)_____

6.)_____

7.)_____

8.)_____

9.)_____

10.)_____

Ethics and Morality

Should cloning plants be legal?
[   ]yes [   ]no

Should cloning animals be legal?
[   ]yes [   ]no

Should cloning humans be legal?
[   ]yes [   ]no

You'd say on average that you lie this many times per day:

_____

If you were impregnated due to rape, would you have an abortion?
[   ]yes [   ]no

Should the number of children a single household has be limited?
[   ]yes [   ]no

If yes, how many children should be allowed per household?

_____

Should people be free to practice any religion they please?
[   ]yes [   ]no

Should prostitution be legal?
[   ]yes [   ]no

If you were a killer, you'd most likely target what sort of people?

_____

Do you believe certain things are impossible?
[   ]yes [   ]no

Do you believe something can be perfect?
[   ]yes [   ]no

Ethics and Morality

Should gambling be legal?

[   ]yes [   ]no

If everyone on the planet worked harder than you and did more good deeds than you, would you consider yourself evil?

[   ]yes [   ]no

Should gay marriage be legal?

[   ]yes [   ]no

Do you think artificial intelligence would spell the end of humanity?

[   ]yes [   ]no

Should abortion be legal?

[   ]yes [   ]no

Should marijuana be legal?

[   ]yes [   ]no

Should slavery be a penalty enforced for breaking certain laws?

[   ]yes [   ]no

Should there be a penalty or fee of some sort for not recycling?

[   ]yes [   ]no

Should torture be a legal form of interrogation?

[   ]yes [   ]no

Should torture be a legal form of punishment?

[   ]yes [   ]no

Would you eat human flesh if your survival depended upon it?

[   ]yes [   ]no

Should nuclear weapons be banished worldwide?

[   ]yes [   ]no

Have you ever felt sympathy for a murderer?

[   ]yes [   ]no

Would you save the lives of 10 Americans over the lives of 100 people from other countries?

[   ]yes [   ]no

Do you believe there would be no morality without religion?

[   ]yes [   ]no

When Someone Says, You Think...

Posters

_____

Purpose

_____

Pyramids

_____

Quarters

_____

Quilts

_____

Rafts

_____

Rain

_____

Rainbows

_____

Rhymes

_____

Rice

_____

Rings

_____

Rivers

_____

Rocks

_____

Rope

_____

Sand

_____

Satin

_____

When Someone Says, You Think...

Scarves

_____

Screens

_____

Seeds

_____

Shadows

_____

Silk

_____

Skipping

_____

Sleep

_____

Sleeves

_____

Slime

_____

Smoke

_____

Snow

_____

Soap

_____

Socks

_____

Spinning

_____

Stairs

_____

Stamps

_____

Your Views On Conspiracy Theories

The cure for cancer is known, and just hasn't
been made available to the public.

    [   ]true [   ]false

    The 9/11 tragedy was planned by the American government.

    [   ]true [   ]false

A civilization more technical than our own existed
at some point in time and has been covered up.

    [   ]true [   ]false

The abduction phenomenon is real and being
covered up by the government.

    [   ]true [   ]false

A small group of very wealthy individuals control the world.

    [   ]true [   ]false

Princess Diana was murdered by the British secret services.

    [   ]true [   ]false

The Earth's first nuclear explosion occurred in Tunguska in 1908;
the result of a nuclear-powered alien spacecraft crashing.

    [   ]true [   ]false

A secret government agency, known as the Men In Black,
exist to discredit any individual claiming to have
experiences with alien beings or spacecraft.

    [   ]true [   ]false

AIDS was purposely introduced.

    [   ]true [   ]false

The Iraq war was orchestrated by extremely rich
Americans to protect their money in oil.

    [   ]true [   ]false

The Knights Templar existed to protect
the secret bloodline of Jesus Christ.

    [   ]true [   ]false

Every move we make is monitored by the government.

    [   ]true [   ]false

At Random

Has anyone written a song about you?
[   ]yes [   ]no

                    Can you bake bread?
                    [   ]yes [   ]no

Do you bruise easily?
[   ]yes [   ]no

                    Have you visited a psychiatrist?
                    [   ]yes [   ]no

Can you do the splits?
[   ]yes [   ]no

                    Do you like to swim?
                    [   ]yes [   ]no

Have you been in a fist fight?
[   ]yes [   ]no

Which one of the following do you believe is the biggest injustice:
___Disability discrimination
___Gender discrimination
___Racial discrimination
___Sexual orientation discrimination

                    Do you like seeing yourself in mirrors?
                    [   ]yes [   ]no
Have you seriously considered joining the military?
[   ]yes [   ]no
    Would you mind if your best friend and your ex began dating?
                    [   ]yes [   ]no
Have you waxed any part of your body?
[   ]yes [   ]no
    Are you sometimes afraid to open your eyes in the dark?
                    [   ]yes [   ]no
Do you believe prayer works?
[   ]yes [   ]no

                    Have you changed a tire?
                    [   ]yes [   ]no

Your Lists

Things you like to do on your days off:

1.)_____

2.)_____

3.)_____

4.)_____

5.)_____

6.)_____

7.)_____

8.)_____

9.)_____

10.)_____

Things which make a good parent:

1.)_____

2.)_____

3.)_____

4.)_____

5.)_____

6.)_____

7.)_____

8.)_____

9.)_____

10.)_____

Your Lists

Things you fear about getting old:

1.)_____
2.)_____
3.)_____
4.)_____
5.)_____
6.)_____
7.)_____
8.)_____
9.)_____
10.)_____

Things you hate which others seem to love:

1.)_____
2.)_____
3.)_____
4.)_____
5.)_____
6.)_____
7.)_____
8.)_____
9.)_____
10.)_____

At Random

Have you talked on the phone for more than six consecutive hours?
    [   ]yes [   ]no

                    Have you hidden under your bedsheets?
                    [   ]yes [   ]no

Have you ridden a mechanical bull?
    [   ]yes [   ]no

                    Have you shaved your eyebrows off?
                    [   ]yes [   ]no

Have you debated in front of a crowd?
    [   ]yes [   ]no

                    Have you seen a UFO?
                    [   ]yes [   ]no

Have you been baptized?
    [   ]yes [   ]no

                    Have you been inside of a confessional booth?
                    [   ]yes [   ]no

Have you bailed someone out of jail?
    [   ]yes [   ]no

                    Have you been robbed?
                    [   ]yes [   ]no

Have you run out of gas while on the road?
    [   ]yes [   ]no

                    Have you sucked helium out of a balloon?
                    [   ]yes [   ]no

Have you put underwear on your head?
    [   ]yes [   ]no

                    Have you jumped off the roof of a house?
                    [   ]yes [   ]no

Have you slept with a stuffed animal in your bed
since reaching the age of 16?
    [   ]yes [   ]no

                    Have you had a hickey?
                    [   ]yes [   ]no

Have you visited someone in jail?
    [   ]yes [   ]no

At Random

Have you been solicited by a prostitute?

    [   ]yes [   ]no

                        Have you been skinny-dipping?

                            [   ]yes [   ]no

Have you been to a strip club?

    [   ]yes [   ]no

                        Have you been attracted to a friend's parent?

                            [   ]yes [   ]no

Have you looked at nude photos of a celebrity?

    [   ]yes [   ]no

                        Have you been on a cruise ship?

                            [   ]yes [   ]no

Have you truly believed you were about to die?

    [   ]yes [   ]no

                    Have you used the sun to reference your direction?

                            [   ]yes [   ]no

Have you been on an airplane?

    [   ]yes [   ]no

                        Have you fallen asleep in a classroom?

                            [   ]yes [   ]no

Have you been a designated driver?

    [   ]yes [   ]no

                            Have you won a contest?

                            [   ]yes [   ]no

Have you had lice?

    [   ]yes [   ]no

                            Have you mowed a lawn?

                            [   ]yes [   ]no

Have you owned a public library card?

    [   ]yes [   ]no

                            Have you taken a drug test?

                            [   ]yes [   ]no

Have you gone more than a week without watching TV?

    [   ]yes [   ]no

                            Have you fainted?

                            [   ]yes [   ]no

Your Lists

Things you wanted to be as a child:

1.)_____
2.)_____
3.)_____
4.)_____
5.)_____
6.)_____
7.)_____
8.)_____
9.)_____
10.)_____

Your biggest life goals:

1.)_____
2.)_____
3.)_____
4.)_____
5.)_____
6.)_____
7.)_____
8.)_____
9.)_____
10.)_____

Your Lists

Things you keep in boxes:

1.)_____

2.)_____

3.)_____

4.)_____

5.)_____

6.)_____

7.)_____

8.)_____

9.)_____

10.)_____

The coolest street names you've encountered:

1.)_____

2.)_____

3.)_____

4.)_____

5.)_____

6.)_____

7.)_____

8.)_____

9.)_____

10.)_____

Superstitions

Do you believe a unified world government
signals the end of the our species?
    [   ]yes [   ]no

Would you feel uneasy if a candle went out
without human interaction?
[   ]yes [   ]no

Do you ever cross your fingers when you wish, hope or lie?
    [   ]yes [   ]no

Do you ever kiss the clock when it reaches a certain time?
[   ]yes [   ]no

Do you believe you must bless someone after they sneeze, because
their heart skips a beat and it might stop altogether otherwise?
    [   ]yes [   ]no

Do you ever pick a seeded dandelion and try to blow
all the seeds off in an effort to make a wish come true?
[   ]yes [   ]no

Do you ever place a fallen eyelash between your thumb and
forefinger, guess at which finger it will be on when you pull your
fingers apart, and then make a wish if you guessed correctly?
    [   ]yes [   ]no

Do you knock on wood for luck?
[   ]yes [   ]no

Do you believe that dreaming of fish means
someone you know is pregnant?
    [   ]yes [   ]no

Do you believe it unlucky to take a shot of liquor without first
tapping the shot glass on a countertop?
[   ]yes [   ]no

Do you believe it unlucky to have a funeral on a Friday?
    [   ]yes [   ]no

Do you believe that whoever catches the bride's bouquet
will be the next to marry?
[   ]yes [   ]no

Do you believe that killing a cat will bring 17 years of bad luck
to the person who does the killing?
    [   ]yes [   ]no

Superstitions

Would you feel compelled to throw money into a fountain or well
and make a wish if you came across one?
    [   ]yes [   ]no
Would you feel uneasy falling asleep with your feet uncovered?
    [   ]yes [   ]no

Do you believe the four of clubs is an
unlucky card to have in your hand?
    [   ]yes [   ]no
Do you believe you can know how many children you will have
by cutting an apple in half and counting the seeds?
    [   ]yes [   ]no

Do you make a wish when you see a shooting star?
    [   ]yes [   ]no
Do you believe that when crossing railroad tracks
you should touch a screw for luck?
    [   ]yes [   ]no

Does the number '666' make you uncomfortable?
    [   ]yes [   ]no
When fishing, do you throw back your first catch, believing
it will make you more likely to continue catching fish?
    [   ]yes [   ]no

Would you be afraid to swallow watermelon seeds for fear
that a watermelon might grow in your stomach?
    [   ]yes [   ]no
Do you believe that if you use the same pencil for taking a test
which you used for studying, there's a likelihood you'll score
better; because the pencil remembers the answers?
    [   ]yes [   ]no

Would you be afraid to take flowers from someone's grave,
because it might mean you'll be the next to die?
    [   ]yes [   ]no
Do you believe you can tell the sex of a child
before birth by whether or not the moon is shining
when the labor contractions begin?
    [   ]yes [   ]no

Would you feel uneasy getting out of bed left foot first?
    [   ]yes [   ]no

Your Lists

Your hobbies:

1.)_____
2.)_____
3.)_____
4.)_____
5.)_____
6.)_____
7.)_____
8.)_____
9.)_____
10.)_____

Things you pride yourself on:

1.)_____
2.)_____
3.)_____
4.)_____
5.)_____
6.)_____
7.)_____
8.)_____
9.)_____
10.)_____

Your Lists

Things you spend your extra money on:

1.)_____
2.)_____
3.)_____
4.)_____
5.)_____
6.)_____
7.)_____
8.)_____
9.)_____
10.)_____

Commonly held beliefs you don't buy into:

1.)_____
2.)_____
3.)_____
4.)_____
5.)_____
6.)_____
7.)_____
8.)_____
9.)_____
10.)_____

At Random

You want your epitaph to read:

_____

_____

The most hurtful thing anyone's ever said to you:

_____

_____

How you honestly feel about the way your parents raised you:

_____

_____

The happiest you've ever been:

_____

_____

What you'd really like to say to telemarketers:

_____

_____

A sport you'd like to see created and played:

_____

_____

What do you hope does not happen when you die?

_____

_____

What drugs would you try if there were no detriments
to your health?

_____

_____

At Random

Something about human anatomy you'd change:

_____

You like for your home to smell like:

_____

How long can you run flat out without stopping?

_____

What color are the underwear you're currently wearing?

_____

Your height:

_____

The height you'd like to be:

_____

What type of milk do you prefer?

_____

You think children are:

_____

You'd like to live to be this age:

_____

The fastest you've ever driven:

_____

How old were you when you stopped believing in Santa Claus?

_____

Your Lists

Some extinct animals you'd bring back to life:

1.)_____
2.)_____
3.)_____
4.)_____
5.)_____
6.)_____
7.)_____
8.)_____
9.)_____
10.)_____

Things you were punished for as a child:

1.)_____
2.)_____
3.)_____
4.)_____
5.)_____
6.)_____
7.)_____
8.)_____
9.)_____
10.)_____

Your Lists

People you dream about:

1.) _____
2.) _____
3.) _____
4.) _____
5.) _____
6.) _____
7.) _____
8.) _____
9.) _____
10.) _____

Facts which amaze you:

1.) _____
2.) _____
3.) _____
4.) _____
5.) _____
6.) _____
7.) _____
8.) _____
9.) _____
10.) _____

Your Least Favorites

Age:

_____

Curse word:

_____

Day of the week:

_____

Exercise:

_____

Firework:

_____

Kind of pillow:

_____

Letter of the alphabet:

_____

Liquor:

_____

Mode of travel:

_____

Month of the year:

_____

Part of a playground:

_____

Piece of clothing:

_____

Planet:

_____

Season:

_____

Sport:

_____

Subject in school:

_____

Time of day:

_____

Type of food:

_____

THIS or THAT

Waffles	___OR___	Pancakes
School	___OR___	Church
Head first	___OR___	Feet first
Truth	___OR___	Dare
Salt	___OR___	Pepper
Predictable	___OR___	Spontaneous
Emotional pain	___OR___	Physical pain
Sneeze	___OR___	Cough
Forests	___OR___	Fields
Snakes	___OR___	Spiders
Fruits	___OR___	Vegetables
Rainbows	___OR___	Shooting stars
Lunar eclipse	___OR___	Solar eclipse
Bubbles	___OR___	Balloons
Business	___OR___	Casual
Stripes	___OR___	Polka dots
Sausage	___OR___	Bacon
Massage	___OR___	Sleep
Tan	___OR___	Pale
Manicure	___OR___	Pedicure
Quiet	___OR___	Loud
Glasses	___OR___	Contacts
Sunblock	___OR___	Tanning oil
Scrambled	___OR___	Fried
Cowboys	___OR___	Indians
Young	___OR___	Old
Stickers	___OR___	Stamps
Visual learner	___OR___	Auditory learner
Test the water	___OR___	Dive in
Tattoos	___OR___	Piercings
Safety	___OR___	Danger
Cursive	___OR___	Print

Your Lists

The worst names to have:

1.)_____
2.)_____
3.)_____
4.)_____
5.)_____
6.)_____
7.)_____
8.)_____
9.)_____
10.)_____

Future inventions you hope for:

1.)_____
2.)_____
3.)_____
4.)_____
5.)_____
6.)_____
7.)_____
8.)_____
9.)_____
10.)_____

Your Lists

Gifts you'd enjoy getting:

1.)_____
2.)_____
3.)_____
4.)_____
5.)_____
6.)_____
7.)_____
8.)_____
9.)_____
10.)_____

Things you wouldn't do for a billion dollars:

1.)_____
2.)_____
3.)_____
4.)_____
5.)_____
6.)_____
7.)_____
8.)_____
9.)_____
10.)_____

Would You Do It For A Billion Dollars?

Let a bee sting you every day of your life?

    [   ]yes [   ]no

               Drink disease-free human blood?

                   [   ]yes [   ]no

Allow scientists to clone you?

    [   ]yes [   ]no

              Let someone cut one of your feet off?

                   [   ]yes [   ]no

Lose the ability to speak indefinitely?

    [   ]yes [   ]no

        Spend a year in complete darkness and solitude?

                   [   ]yes [   ]no

Purposely gain 500 pounds?

    [   ]yes [   ]no

             Tattoo Hitler's name on your forehead?

                   [   ]yes [   ]no

Destroy the pyramids of Giza?

    [   ]yes [   ]no

        Spend a week alone in a room full of dead bodies?

                   [   ]yes [   ]no

Be confined to a third world country
for the next ten years of your life?

    [   ]yes [   ]no

            Pee on a stranger every day of your life?

                   [   ]yes [   ]no

Lose your ability to orgasm indefinitely?

    [   ]yes [   ]no

       Never again be able to speak to or see anyone you know?

                   [   ]yes [   ]no

Let someone cut one of your hands off?

    [   ]yes [   ]no

   Walk naked through a mile of dirty diapers piled up to your neck?

                   [   ]yes [   ]no

Dig someone out of their grave, remove all
of their clothes, and rebury them?

    [   ]yes [   ]no

Would You Do It For A Billion Dollars?

Be put to death 25 years from today's date?

[   ]yes [   ]no

    Let someone brand twenty random symbols onto your back?

               [   ]yes [   ]no

Never again be allowed more than six hours of sleep
in a 24 hour period?

[   ]yes [   ]no

    Spend half an hour in a tank containing a live giant squid?

               [   ]yes [   ]no

Let someone paralyze you from the waist down?

[   ]yes [   ]no

    Bleed from your mouth, nose, eyes and ears for ten minutes
daily for the rest of your life?

               [   ]yes [   ]no

Have to live with a lion's tail surgically implanted
directly above your rear?

[   ]yes [   ]no

    Let someone drown you and successfully bring you back to life?

               [   ]yes [   ]no

Never be able to have or adopt children?

[   ]yes [   ]no

    Lose all memory of your life prior to this moment?

               [   ]yes [   ]no

Swallow 1000 quarters in a 24 hour period?

[   ]yes [   ]no

    Let someone shoot you ten times in places
which wouldn't kill or disable you?

               [   ]yes [   ]no

Never again be allowed to consume
more than 1000 calories per day?

[   ]yes [   ]no

               Eat a live frog?

               [   ]yes [   ]no

When Someone Says, You Think...

Stars

_____

Statues

_____

Steam

_____

Streetlights

_____

Stretches

_____

Stripes

_____

Strobes

_____

Suitcases

_____

Sunglasses

_____

Sunlight

_____

Sunrises

_____

Sunsets

_____

Surprises

_____

Sweat

_____

Tears

_____

Theaters

_____

When Someone Says, You Think...

Thorns

_____

Thunder

_____

Ties

_____

Toboggans

_____

Trampolines

_____

Trees

_____

Umbrellas

_____

Violins

_____

War

_____

Waterbeds

_____

Waterfalls

_____

Waves

_____

Wheels

_____

Whistle

_____

Wind

_____

Zippers

_____

At Random

What's the longest amount of time you'd date someone before giving up on the idea of them committing?

_____

Have you taken an IQ test?
    [   ]yes [   ]no

        Have you seen a shooting star?
           [   ]yes [   ]no

Pizza toppings you like:

___Anchovies	___Mushrooms
___Bacon	___Olives
___Belle peppers	___Onions
___Canadian bacon	___Pepperoni
___Chicken	___Pineapple
___Hamburger	___Sausage
___Jalapenos	___Spinach

One bad thing you think an ex might have to say about you:

_____

One good thing you think an ex might have to say about you:

_____

Do you think pregnancy is beautiful?
    [   ]yes [   ]no

        Can you put your feet behind your head?
           [   ]yes [   ]no

Do clowns scare you?
    [   ]yes [   ]no

Can you say the alphabet backwards without referencing it?
           [   ]yes [   ]no

What is the purpose of life?

_____

At Random

How many times have you been in love?

_____

Do you like to dance?
    [   ]yes [   ]no

                                     Can you carry a tune?
                                  [   ]yes [   ]no

You'd rather never have to do which one of the following again:
___Brush your teeth   ___Laundry and dishes
___Fix and wash your hair   ___Shave any part of your body

Your porn star name would be:

_____

You believe which one of the following statements to be the truest:
___There are no coincidences
___Everything is a matter of chance
___It's all about balance
___There's no point in thinking about these sorts of things

If humans went extinct, which animal do you think would someday attain consciousness and take over the planet?

_____

Which one of the following options would you prefer:
___Living deep underground   ___Living on another planet
___Living on a space station   ___Living under an ocean
___Living on an island in the sky

Would you bring dinosaurs back from extinction if you could?
    [   ]yes [   ]no
            Do you believe that you could live happily without sex?
                                  [   ]yes [   ]no

Your Lists

Celebrities you're attracted to:

1.)_____
2.)_____
3.)_____
4.)_____
5.)_____
6.)_____
7.)_____
8.)_____
9.)_____
10.)_____

Foreign words you adore:

1.)_____
2.)_____
3.)_____
4.)_____
5.)_____
6.)_____
7.)_____
8.)_____
9.)_____
10.)_____

Your Lists

Amazing epitaphs you've come across:

1.)_____
2.)_____
3.)_____
4.)_____
5.)_____
6.)_____
7.)_____
8.)_____
9.)_____
10.)_____

Songs you want played at your funeral:

1.)_____
2.)_____
3.)_____
4.)_____
5.)_____
6.)_____
7.)_____
8.)_____
9.)_____
10.)_____

Before You Die, You'd Like To...

1.) _____

2.) _____

3.) _____

4.) _____

5.) _____

6.) _____

7.) _____

8.) _____

9.) _____

10.) _____

11.) _____

12.) _____

13.) _____

14.) _____

15.) _____

16.) _____

17.) _____

Before You Die, You'd Like To…

18.)_____

19.)_____

20.)_____

21.)_____

22.)_____

23.)_____

24.)_____

25.)_____

26.)_____

27.)_____

28.)_____

29.)_____

30.)_____

31.)_____

32.)_____

33.)_____

34.)_____

Before You Die, You'd Like To...

35.)_____

36.)_____

37.)_____

38.)_____

39.)_____

40.)_____

41.)_____

42.)_____

43.)_____

44.)_____

45.)_____

In the event of your death, you want this journal given to:

_____

Your signature: Date completed:

_____   _____

THE EXPERIENCE DOESN'T END HERE

Complete your collection of The Secret Me books today
by purchasing any of the following online.

The Secret Me:

A Biased Perspective

A Companion's Relic

A Companion's Relic (the naming edition)

A Couch Potato's Take (table game edition)

A Couch Potato's Take (television edition)

A Couch Potato's Take (video game edition)

A Couple's Inquiry

A Fantasy Manifesto

A Film Fanatic's Record

A Harry Potter Examination

A List Lover's Keepsake

A Music Enthusiast's Diary (1-2)

A Music Enthusiast's Diary (the unguided edition)

A Nonsense Adventure

A Questionnaire Journal (1-2)

A Questionnaire Journal for Teens

A Rated Survey (1-3)

A Shared Life Log (1-2)

Most every book in the series can be obtained online for under $10!
They ship fast, and often free, from the world's
most trusted book source.

Made in the USA
San Bernardino, CA
08 March 2016